PURGATORY

AND

HEAVEN

by

J. P. ARENDZEN, D.D.

TAN Books
An Imprint of Saint Benedict Press, LLC
Charlotte, North Carolina

Nihil obstat: John A. Goodwine, J.C.D.
                  Censor librorum

Imprimatur: ✠ Frances Cardinal Spellman
                  Archbishop of New York
                  January 15, 1960

From *What Becomes of the Dead?* by J. P. Arendzen.

Copyright 1951 by Sheed & Ward, Inc.

Reprinted by TAN Books, an Imprint of Saint Benedict Press, LLC, under agreement with Sheed & Ward, Inc.

Library of Congress Catalog Card Number: 60-7317.

ISBN: 978-0-89555-045-3

Cover design by Tony Pro.

Cover image: *The Holy Mass of Father Stanislaus Papczynski*. Painting by Father Jan Niezabitowski, end of the 18th century, in the chapel of the Marian Fathers in Skórzec.

TAN Books
An Imprint of Saint Benedict Press, LLC
Charlotte, North Carolina
2012

Contents

PURGATORY AND HEAVEN

PURGATORY AND HEAVEN

1. Judgment at Death

IT IS appointed unto men once to die, and after that the Judgment. So we read in the Epistle to the Hebrews (ix. 27). We are willing to be absent from our body and to be at home with the Lord, for we must all be made manifest before the Judgment Seat of Christ: that each one may receive the things done in the body, according to what he has done, whether it be good or bad. So we read in the Second Epistle to the Corinthians (v. 8-10). "The time of my departure is come. I have fought the good fight, I have finished the course, I have kept the faith: henceforth there is laid up for me the crown of righteousness which the Lord, the righteous Judge, shall give to me at that day" (II Tim. iv. 6-8). "I desire to depart and be with Christ" (Phil. i. 23). So spoke St. Paul at the end of his life.

Thus the Scriptures teach that when we are divested of this body, we are with Christ, unless indeed we must suffer a temporary delay in attaining the vision of God, or have chosen everlasting exile from His glory. The Church, therefore, has always taught that death is immediately followed by a Divine Judgment on the departed. No sooner has the soul left the body, but, if it was in mortal sin, it is in hell; if it was without any stain or remnant of sin, it is in heaven; if it was in sanctifying grace, but with stains and remnants of sin, it is in purgatory. This necessitates a Divine Judgment on the state of the departed soul.

Now, this Judgment considered in God Himself is merely that infinite unchanging act which is both His Wisdom and His own very being. It is that knowledge by which He within His own Self infallibly knows the exact state of every departing soul.

God's judgment, however, viewed from our standpoint, from the standpoint of those who undergo it, is a manifestation to us of the truth of God's verdict.

The Judgment immediately after death in consequence consists of the intense and vivid realisation of *three* things: our true moral state as the outcome of all the free acts during our mortal life; secondly, the appropriateness and inevitableness of our future lot whatever it be, and lastly the presence of that Personal Being, that Individual Intelligence to whom we are responsible and who now justly carries out His will upon us. We shall know our past life, the justice of our present lot, and the presence of a Divine Judge.

We shall instantaneously know our past life as we have never known it before. In this life one of the most terrible consequences of sins is that we are apt to forget them. A strange imperfection which accompanies our best acts is that we overvalue them. A constant weakness in our estimate of our past actions is that we misjudge them. A sad condition of our present state of trial is that even the good are not certain with infallible certainty whether they are worthy of love or hatred; they have to work out their salvation in fear and trembling (Phil. ii. 12).

The moment after death the soul sees itself even as it is. Interests which seemed overpowering during our mortal life dwindle into insignificance, and so-called trifles stand out in immense importance. The glamour of earthly praise or blame, and the merely human standards of honour and dishonour are scorned for their ludicrous inadequacy, when the cold, steady, white light of the Sun of infinite Righteousness shines on our past. For some no doubt it will be as if they were members of a theatre troupe, who in their tinsel and tawdry finery suddenly stepped from the artificial footlights into the blazing light of a summer's day at noontide. For some no doubt, who in fear and trembling worked out their salvation and who with anxious scrutiny examined and weighed their deeds, despairing of themselves and only trusting in the mercy of God, for them it will be like passing from the twilight of a winter's day into the clarity of a morning in spring.

The searchlight of God shall illumine the deepest
depths of the human soul, and nothing shall be
hidden that shall not be made manifest to it. Irresistible conviction will grip and hold the soul and in
unshakeable certainty it will realise: Such, then,
am I!

The second point the departed will realise is the
justice of their future lot. The instant after death the
damned will be convinced that hell is the only possibility for them. It stands written of Judas: he went
unto his own place (Acts iii. 25). Thus even if the
verdict be not audibly pronounced at the Particular
Judgment, an overwhelming force from within will
lead the damned to their own place. No mental
questioning arises, no doubt whatever is possible,
the absolute justice flashes upon them with the
swiftness of lightning: they must go to their own
place.

None of the damned have ever asked for mercy,
nor will they for all eternity. One moment's repentance would empty hell. The damned know it, but
nothing alters their grim determination to abide by
their choice and do without God. Hell is the outcome of the rejection of divine Power, Wisdom and
Love, by created wills fixed in evil. Herein then, lies
the mystery, in the fact that the human will is such
that it can be fixed in evil, that it becomes deter-

mined, stark and stiff in its final choice of self as
against God.

The lot of the saved, though in total contrast with
that of the lost, will in this be the same, that it
exactly corresponds with their holy state and the
Saints will know it. True, their state is the outcome
of Divine grace, but given it to be what it is, their
place is with God. As the iron flies to the magnet,
so will they fly to the bosom of God. They may in
life have sinned through frailty, but through God's
grace they have so repented that no remnant of sin,
no stain or debt whatever, remains. God makes them
utter their own sentence, and out of their own
mouths He will happily judge them. They see themselves utterly cleansed, perfect and holy, and will
with blissful boldness dare to say: Heaven is ours!
God will echo the sentence: Heaven is yours!

Newman in *The Dream of Gerontius* describes
the thoughts of the departed who for a while are
bidden to be purified in purgatory. He describes how
the loving sentence of God is carried out spontaneously, nay, eagerly, by those Holy Souls; they know
in their innermost selves that heaven is not yet for
such as they. Willingly do they descend into their
depth of sorrow, where they can weep and wait
till their eyes can bear the effulgence of the Divine
Light.

The third fact known to the departed, without

which the beginning of their eternity would not be
a judgment at all, is the presence of the Judge. God
is not an abstraction, not even abstract holiness or
justice. God is a living, personal, infinite Spirit.
Death is the meeting of our spirit with His. This can
only be by some Divine manifestation of His Presence beyond what we realise by our unaided reason
on earth. It is not only a judgment we shall hear, it
is a Judge we shall face. After the very instant of our
death we shall know ourselves in the immediate
presence of Someone, whose reality shall be closer
to us than any fellowship has ever been to us in this
world, Someone of dread sanctity and boundless
power, Someone unutterably stern yet kind, Someone, whose thought searches us through and through
and from whom it would be folly to hide, Someone
on whom our eternal fate depends, Someone infinitely great, before whom we are infinitesimally
small, Someone who can do with us as He lists. That
Someone the damned will instantaneously recoil
from in hate. That Someone the souls destined for
purgatory will humbly adore and sorrowfully leave
for a while. Only to the Saints will that first sight be
the Beatific Vision of God as He is, to all others it
will be some manifestation less than Himself, but
none the less a display of His Presence exceeding
any experience on earth. The moment after death
everyone stands before the Judge. It has been asked

whether at that moment it will be God in His divine nature only or Christ, God made man, who will be our Judge even in His human nature.

Doubtless it will be Christ, for the Father hath given all judgment to the Son, say the Scriptures, and it is meet and just that men should receive their judgment from the Man Christ Jesus.

Thus at death the just shall forthwith be brought into the immediate presence of Him whose precious blood purchased for them so great salvation. The damned shall face Him, whom, as the Scriptures say, they have crucified afresh by their sins.

Those who shortly before death received the Viaticum of the Body and Blood of Christ shall exchange His Real Presence in the Blessed Sacrament for a Presence, not less real though less hidden, of the same Christ come to judgment. Those who have never known or have rejected the loving mystery of the altar, shall after death bend their knees for the first time to the Man of Nazareth, the nearness of whose Majesty they cannot doubt or deny.

At a Catholic deathbed the words of the priest saying the Commendation of the Departing Soul will not long wait for their fulfilment. He will pray over the dying man: "May the gentle and joyful countenance of Christ Jesus appear unto thee."

It may indeed be asked whether Our Lord will be perceived in bodily form by the disembodied soul

at the Judgment. If the Judgment immediately pre-
cedes entrance into heaven, this cannot reasonably
be doubted. In any case the awareness of this human
presence can be brought about within the disembodied soul in a way which we at present cannot
describe. The Saints in their ecstasies were often in
intercourse with Our Blessed Lord, irresistibly certain of this immediate nearness without, however,
having any bodily vision.

The imagination of the faithful has often pictured
the meeting of the soul with Jesus in Particular
Judgment. Some have dwelt especially on the
thought that these two, Jesus and the person to be
judged, shall be alone together; others again have
imagined the assistance of the defending and the ac-
cusing angel, of the angel guardian and the devil at
this momentous interview. In truth, we know but
little of these things, though we may guess much.
The presence of the angels at the Judgment seems
to have some support from the liturgy, in which the
office of ushering in the souls to God's presence is
attributed to them. Every priest remembers the
prayer at the Offertory in the Requiem Mass: "May
the standard-bearer Michael usher them in to the
holy light." Whether, however, these and many other
beautiful liturgical prayers refer to the moment of
judgment or of final entrance into heaven is difficult
to say.

The prayer of the Church for the departing soul has a grandeur, a tenderness and a soul-stirring vividness, which no one who has ever read it can ever forget. "At the departure of thy soul from the body may the glorious choir of Angels meet thee," prays the Church over the dying. If we find it difficult to realise that such great supernatural solemnity should attend a humble deathbed, we should recall to mind that the King of Kings Himself attends each deathbed when He is received in Holy Communion and when through the ministry of His priests He anoints the senses of the dying and seals them unto life everlasting. When we ponder these things, no solemnity attending the Judgment would seem too great, and the room where a person has died is invested with a strange glory as the place where great scenes have taken place.

2. Purgatory

ST. CATHERINE of Genoa, shortly before the Reformation which rejected the belief in purgatory with scorn, wrote on purgatory the most sublime treatise we possess. In this treatise she wrote:

"Apart from the happiness of the saints in heaven, I think there is no joy comparable to that of the souls in purgatory. An incessant communication with God renders their happiness daily more intense, and this union with God grows more and more intimate, according as the impediments to that union, which exist in the soul, are consumed. These obstacles are the rust and the remains, as it were, of sin; and the fire continues to consume them, and thus the soul gradually expands under the divine influence. Thus, according as the rust diminishes and the soul is laid bare to the divine rays, happiness is augmented. The one grows and the other wanes until the time of trial is elapsed. Yet the pain is not lessened, it is only the time of suffering which decreases. With regard to the will of these souls, they can never say that these pains are pains, so great is their contentment with the ordinance of God, with which their wills are united in perfect charity."

So far St. Catherine. Her words need but little explanation. The state of the Holy Souls can be summed up in the words: an intense unsatisfied desire to see God. Now all desire, while it remains unsatisfied, constitutes pain of some kind and brings some sort of sadness. Desire with certainty of never being satisfied is intense torture. Its pain is in proportion to the realisation of the greatness of the good ultimately lost and our responsibility in having lost it.

Desire without certainty of ever being satisfied is pain mixed with the sweetness of hope.

Desire with the absolute certainty of being satisfied is both joy and pain. Both pain and joy increase equally in proportion to the realisation of the good to be attained and of our own responsibility in having merited both its ultimate attainment and its present delay.

The Holy Souls are inexpressibly happy and inexpressibly sad. They are happy because by God's grace and their own free will they have secured the certainty of seeing and enjoying Him, whom they supremely love. They are sad because through their own fault they are deprived of the blissful vision of His glory

(2) THE STILLNESS OF PURGATORY

Purgatory, not unlike heaven, is a place of rest. All the petty anxieties of life have gone. All unruly cravings and longings have gone. We have worked out our salvation in fear and trembling, but we know we are saved; all our fear and uncertainty about our final end has gone. The dread of death has gone, for that great ordeal is over and lies behind us. The multitudinous interests of earthly life, with its annoyances and pains, are gone. The soul is no longer in contact with material things, for its body is gone. It may be in touch with some of the people on earth, but this is only indirectly through the kindness of God, who reveals it to us, and only in the measure in which He does so. These souls may pray for the ones they left behind, and God will hear them, but it will be like the prayer of the saints, it will be in utmost submission to the will of God, without disturbance or disappointment. All possible friction with our fellow-men is gone, for our fellows in purgatory are in complete harmony with us, each pursuing his own path Godward. No cell in a monastery more tranquil, no seclusion in a convent more absolute, than our stillness in purgatory. We are just left with God alone.

Our resignation to our lot is not merely complete, it is loving, it is affectionate. We are "Holy Souls" and love Him with greater intensity than we have ever done on earth. In our utter solitude we turn the steady gaze of our mind in one direction—towards the dawn. Perhaps no two words will better describe what purgatory must be than stillness and twilight. This twilight will be the deeper the farther we are away from God, the longer our stay in that realm of shadows. But it will never be a realm of ghosts, for there is no terror or dread of the unknown, no shuddering at the unsuspected power of evil. There will be no sin, and therefore no danger from the Evil One can ever befall us. We are the children of God and eternally safe. "The souls of the saints are in the hands of God."

Yet purgatory is a place of untold sorrow. The flames of purgatory may be metaphorical, but they are at least a metaphor for a reality which far exceeds mere bodily pain. We commonly speak of a burning desire. Even on earth an unsatisfied desire may become an acute mental pain, a consuming anguish greater than any torture by physical hurt. Even during life our greatest pains are not physical. The loss of a mother, a wife or a child, the loss of honour or goods, the dread of poverty or disgrace, the humiliation by an enemy, the shame before a friend, the fierce pain of a reproach, the sharp word of contempt, the ingratitude of those whom we loved; such things hurt more than any bodily pain.

Such things have brought people to madness or self-destruction; bodily pain but rarely does.

If frustrated desires on earth do not usually inflict such unbearable pain, it is because the objects of our desires are not often so great. But people have languished and died for love of one another, when cruel fate separated them. "Strong as death is love, and many waters cannot extinguish it," say the Scriptures. On earth we have the power to divert our attention, to seek other interests, to try and desire new and other things; in purgatory not so. In our solitude there will be but one object of desire: God. On earth we find a respite in merciful sleep, but in purgatory there is an incessant and sleepless yearning thought: God! The soul will be set free from the trammels of the body and its power of thinking will be immeasurably greater than here on earth. Here we are dulled by our bodily organism; there the spirit will be free, and the width of its grasp and the clearness of its vision, the penetration of its reason, will be so keen that it will exceed that of the wisest on earth.

As with our knowledge, so with our will. Our hearts will expand and our desires be in extent and intensity beyond what we can now conceive, and all our powers will be focussed on God, and on God alone. Every fibre of our being will thrill at the thought of God, as if, with arms outstretched, we were kneeling before God, imploring and beseeching Him, not in audible words or sighs, but in keen and piercing thoughts, even Him of whom we are deprived.

(3) MENTAL AGONY IN PURGATORY

This will cause acute pain, greater pain than we have ever known; it will be like a sword going right through the heart. Were death still possible we would die for sorrow, but death is over and we have to bear it, till God relieves us. When Christ was in agony in the Garden of Gethsemane, He sweated blood and the drops of His blood fell on the ground. There was then no bodily pain, but only mental sorrow: "My soul is sorrowful unto death," He had said on entering the garden. He writhed in agony, and, prostrate on the ground, He pleaded: "Father, all things are possible unto Thee; let this chalice pass away; yet not My will but Thine be done." A picture indeed of our sorrows in purgatory, when our souls shall be sorrowful unto death, when mere bodily death would be a welcome respite, when we would be willing to die a thousand times if thereby we could reach God one instant sooner.

To cold, calculating souls of to-day this may all seem fanciful and exaggerated, yet so far from fancy or exaggeration is this, that it is only a feeble attempt somehow to express a reality which exceeds

our boldest thoughts. Moreover, the soul realises this
hindrance to the vision of God as a blemish within
itself, a stain clinging to its innermost being. It is
not God who forcibly repels, but a fault and a flaw
within, a darkness and a defilement pervading the
very soul, making it unfit for the all-holy presence of
God; it is a result, a remnant of sin, not totally undone by penance, which creates this impossibility of
approaching God. The fierce light from the throne
of God would shrivel the soul and burn it to ashes—
if such a simile may be used—and the thought of the
clinging presence of this stain is burning pain beyond description. Nothing defiled can enter heaven
(Apoc. xxi. 27). To appear before God in its present state would mean an insult to God, who is supremely loved; even if it were possible, it would
mean immeasurable suffering to the soul not yet
perfect. The exile, in consequence, is accepted willingly, eagerly, in the certainty of ultimate purifica-
tion and final holiness, and as the only means to
purge away the stain.

They lament, but they do not complain. Purgatory is one great *mea maxima culpa,* and a loving glorification of God, who is infinitely just. Thus
God calls the soul to Himself, yet the soul cannot
yet come. Hearing this call, it answers with a flam-
ing desire to leap forward, and yet must remain
away, till the very vehemence and duration of its

holy desires have undone the havoc which sin had wrought. Anyone who has read St. Teresa knows how she continually emphasises the intensity of pain in her highest happiness. The greater her vision or intuition of God, the more fearful her suffering. At first this seems strange and paradoxical till the reader begins to grasp that it must be so. The greater the unfulfilled desire, the greater the pain. Yet this pain, beyond all earthly pain, the souls in purgatory will have to bear until all stain is purged away, unless indeed the Faithful on earth help them by their prayers and hasten their entrance into that Presence, which taketh all sorrow away and fills the human heart with everlasting joy.

(4) THE FIRE OF PURGATORY

Are we bound to believe that the fire of purgatory is physically real in the sense in which the fire of hell is?

It is certainly not an article of Catholic Faith in the technical and formal sense. It has never been defined by the solemn magisterium of the Church, by Pope or Council, and it is at least not obviously taught by the Church's ordinary magisterium. The question of the physical reality of fire in purgatory has, as a matter of fact, been brought before the teaching authority of the Church on historic occa-

sions, and she has apparently deliberately not defined it. The Greeks were held to be unsound in
their belief in purgatory, and hence they were required on reunion with the Church to state definitely
what they believed. Thus the Emperor Michael Pale-
ologus accepted a profession of faith, proposed to
him by Pope Clement IV in 1267, and this Emperor
handed this profession to Gregory X at the Second
Œcumenical Council of Lyons. In it he stated his
belief "that those who after baptism fall into sin . . .
if they depart this life in charity truly penitent, before they have by worthy fruits of penance satisfied
for what they have committed and omitted . . . their
souls are purified by purgatorial or cleansing pains
after death, as Brother John has explained to us."
Pope and Council were satisfied with this declara-
tion; though it was notorious that the Greeks did not
accept the physical reality of purgatorial fire, nothing more was required of them.

When, some two hundred years later, the Greek
Cardinal, Bessarion, at the Council of Florence
argued against the existence of a real fire in purgatory, the Greeks were assured that the Roman
Church had never dogmatically pronounced on this
point, and in the Decree of Union nothing was said
about it. In the Council of Trent nothing whatever
was decreed about the kind of pain in purgatory.

Hence we may take it for granted that the reality of the fire of purgatory is not of Catholic faith.

A further question is whether in addition to the pain of loss there is some pain of the senses, even if the fire be no physical reality. Here again there is no solemn definition on the subject, and it would be hard to prove that the ordinary magisterium teaches anything as divinely revealed in this matter.

It is true that for many centuries in the West in popular addresses to the faithful and in the popular imagination of the people, both the fire and the pain of the senses have been taken for granted, but between this and official Catholic teaching there is a wide margin. It may be asked whence the association of the pain of fire with purgatory at all?

There can be no doubt that the text of St. Paul, 1 Cor. iii. 12, is the historical cause of this association. We read: "No other foundation can any man lay than that which is already laid, which is Jesus Christ. But if a man buildeth upon the foundation, whether it be gold, silver, precious stones, wood, grass or straw, the work of each man shall become manifest. For the Day shall declare it, because that day is to be disclosed in fire, and the worth of each man's work that fire shall assay. If any man's work abide, which he hath built thereon, he shall receive reward: if any man's work be burnt up, he shall suffer loss, but himself shall be saved, yet so as through fire."

From earliest days in East and West the last words "saved yet as through fire" have been understood rightly of a state of ultimate salvation after death, which at the same time was a state of loss or punishment (*zemiothesetai*—he shall be mulcted, punished, fined). Part of this passage is obviously metaphorical, but this does not prove that the final words, "so as through fire," must be. The fire of the Day, of Judgment Day, was certainly not metaphorical in St. Paul's thoughts.

It cannot be gainsaid, therefore, that the Scripture text affords serious grounds for thinking that the cleansing fires are not purely metaphorical. Though in her official and liturgical prayers the Church does not allude to fire in purgatory, the ordinary prayers of the simple faithful for many centuries in the West presuppose fire.

As all sin is not merely a turning away from God but an inordinate turning to and clinging to creatures, it seems in accordance with reason that there should be in addition to the pain of loss, which corresponds to the turning away from God during this life, another suffering corresponding to the inordinate turning towards creatures; that is, some pain of the senses. But as God has not given us any further light of revelation in this matter, even good men have doubted on this point, and it is not ours to lay a burden on the faith of the faithful which the Church does not impose.

Saints may have described visions they had of the flames of purgatory, but Saints, such as St. John in his Revelation in the New Testament, have also described visions of material glories in heaven: golden streets and gates of precious stones, crowns and robes and thrones. No one, however, is bound to believe that these latter are physical material realities as described in the Apocalypse. We cannot claim more for the visions of the Saints than for Holy Writ itself.

(5) COMPARISON BETWEEN HELL AND PURGATORY

It has been said that the pains of purgatory are in all things equal to those of hell, except that the pains of hell are eternal, and those of purgatory only temporal. Hell has the double pain of loss and of sense, therefore also purgatory.

But the saying that the pains of hell and purgatory are the same has to be so hedged round, so modified, so weakened, that it is difficult to see what truth remains in it. Take away the irretrievable alienation from God and the eternity of the punishment from hell, and hell is hell no more. It is the certainty of the eternity of the pains of hell which makes them what they are. The sufferings of the damned, and the sufferings of the Holy Souls, are only analogically the same, nothing more. There seems something incongruous in the thought that God should inflict the same punishment on those who eternally hate Him and are fixed in evil, and also on those who love Him above all things and are destined to be His companions everlastingly. The sameness of punishment can surely not refer to the *poena damni* or the pain of loss, for in the sense in which the damned have lost God, the Holy Souls have not lost Him at all. They possess Him in grace and in love, though not yet in vision. If this sameness of punishment is to refer to the *poena sensus,* the pain of the senses, it must first be established beyond doubt that there is such a pain, and secondly that venial sins, or the remnants of mortal sin, are likely to be punished in the same way as unrepented mortal sin itself.

The only point of identity between hell and purgatory is the fact that the inmates of both are actually without the enjoyment of the vision of God, but so are we also here on earth. If it be argued that both the damned and Holy Souls are without the vision of God *through their own fault,* this must be admitted. As, however, the fault of both is not the same, but differs in kind and not merely in degree, it is only reasonable to suppose that the pain caused by the lack of the vision of God differs in kind as well as in degree.

It is therefore best to avoid an expression which can no doubt be correctly understood after much explanation, but which may give rise to many misunderstandings. To picture purgatory merely as a temporary hell would be a gross error.

(6) THE AVOIDANCE OF PURGATORY

There is, alas, amongst many of the faithful the unreasonable conviction that practically all must after death pass through purgatory, that only the Saints go straight from their deathbed to heaven, that it would be too much to hope and, in fact, presumptuous in the ordinary mortal to expect to escape those cleansing flames. This unreasoned persuasion is nourished by the thought that very holy persons, in fact, the Saints themselves, have asked for prayers after their death, that none of the Saints have dared to claim certainty that they should go straightway to heaven. There is, moreover, an instinctive humility in the hearts of most of the faithful, reminding them of their many sins in the past and their weakness for the future. In consequence they practically take it for granted that they and every ordinary man and woman will have to pass some time in purgatory. To escape purgatory they would consider the highest re-

ward of sanctity, received by practically none but
those whose names appear in the calendar. Though
humility in our own case is a wholesome virtue, it is
none the less true that this taking of purgatory for
granted can, and often does, have a most deleterious
effect.

First of all, it is not true that the avoidance of
purgatory is only the reward of highest sanctity.
Rather it is true to say that the avoidance of purgatory is independent of any particular degree of sanctity. *Not* only exceptionally holy persons avoid
purgatory, *but* also persons who die without venial
sins on their souls and without a debt to pay to God's
justice for sins already forgiven.

Such absence of venial guilt and debt is compati-
ble with much less than the highest degree of sanctity. The degree of sanctity in fact has nothing
directly to do with it. The condition for avoiding
purgatory is a negative, not a positive one; there
must be no sins and no remnants of sin. This negative condition is possible in persons even of lowly at-
tainments in sanctity.

It has been maintained with some show of reason
that a person who died in greater sanctity, with
greater merits to his account and with greater final
glory to come, might pass a longer time in purgatory
than another person, less in grace and in future
glory, but who after a life of sheltered virtue gave up

an innocent soul to God. Innocence and sanctity are not quite convertible terms.

Though it is temerity to speak with too much assurance about these matters, it seems possible for a person to practise even heroic virtues in many ways and yet to have serious faults to account for in other directions. A man may have a rich treasure laid up in heaven and yet have to wait before entering into his inheritance on account of an unpaid debt for forgiven mortal sin, or on account of smaller faults, never deleted by penance. It seems possible to pass from one's deathbed straight to heaven, but to occupy only a lower throne in the realm of light. He that prays for an increase of sanctifying grace prays for a greater thing than he who prays for escape from purgatory.

The Penitent Thief heard the consoling words: "To-day thou shalt be with me in Paradise," but this is no absolute proof that he is one of the highest of God's saints, though a Saint he is. On the other hand it is clear that the more the grace, the greater the means of deleting venial guilt and the debt to God's justice. One act of supreme love would wash away all stains, and grace is but the means of loving God.

We must likewise remember that the baptised infant on death straightway enters glory, but does not necessarily sit higher in God's Kingdom than the adult who passes through purgatory.

Let all this be said only for the purpose of show-
ing that the avoidance of purgatory is not such an
impossible task, not the reward for such exceptional
sanctity, that the ordinary faithful dare not hope for
it. The holy submission to the sorrows of life, the
voluntary acceptance of death and its pains, the little acts of self-sacrifice, acts of charity which cover
a multitude of sins, the use of the Church's power in
indulgences may well enable many of the faithful,
whose names on earth will never be mentioned in
the list of Saints, and who were reputed to be but
humble folk in spiritual things, to pass from death
straight to God.

One may well hope that especially amongst the
poor, who have religiously and patiently borne years
of neglect and distress, especially amongst those to
whom God gave the grace of a long, painful illness to
which they lovingly and meekly submitted, there are
many indeed who after death have no more debt to
pay. Most priests have known instances of simple
people who have borne the long-drawn-out and
agonizing pains of cancer almost without a murmur
or a word of irritation, but in continual, affectionate
and pitiful prayer and utterance of the Holy Name.
In such cases it may well be doubted that God
should continue their pains after death and delay
their eternal reward.

In an old English prayer, which our forefathers loved to use but which is well-nigh forgotten now, there was a petition: Jesus send me here my purgatory. Such a prayer is a genuine utterance of the Catholic faith and encouraged by the Catholic Church. It would not be so if it were a petition for an abnormal thing which was only granted to the highest saints.

The conviction that whatever one might do, purgatory is practically unavoidable, must lame all serious effort to escape it. It is often a sign of a low level of spiritual life, and if fully understood, would be dishonouring to God.

After the death of His only begotten Son, it cannot be practically impossible to lead such a life on earth as would fit us directly for the glory of heaven. It would, moreover, presuppose the gaining of a plenary indulgence during life to be virtually impossible, a thesis which is hard to reconcile with the mind and the practice of the Church.

The more we regard the avoidance of purgatory as an achievement possible even in normal circumstances, possible to the humble and the simple, within the reach of less than the heights of sanctity, the more we shall be spurred on to obtain what we hope to be within our powers. Despondency has brought more people to hell than presumption, and despondency has brought more people to a long stay in purgatory than a loving confidence in the grace of God.

(7) PRAYERS FOR SOULS IN PURGATORY

It has been revealed to us that the Holy Souls can be helped by the prayers and good deeds and the sacrifices of the faithful on earth.

The Holy Souls can merit no more. Nothing they can do can add to their final glory, or can hasten the time for their delivery from purgatory. In a sense, therefore, they are utterly helpless, but they can be helped by others without any merit whatever of their own. This is a great mystery. At first it seems difficult to see how it can be. Some childlike minds just think that the Holy Souls are let off so many days, months or years, and thus enter heaven so much the sooner. This, however, is a very imperfect way of conceiving things.

The Holy Souls could not enter the sight of God before they were inwardly, essentially and intrinsically prepared for it. Even God's mercy would not break the law of heaven, that nothing defiled shall enter therein (Apoc. xxi. 27). If the Holy Souls entered heaven before their time, in the sense that their acceptance of pain had not yet purged their stains away, if God should for some external reason, for someone else's sake, admit them unprepared in His presence, they would beg to return to purgatory, for heaven would not be heaven to them. If then, the faithful can help them with their prayers, they can only do so from within, not from without. There can be no mere extrinsic imputation of merits, as if God pretended for our sakes that the Holy Souls were prepared for His sight, whereas in reality they were not.

A Holy Soul enters heaven only when as a matter of fact it is totally stainless, and not before. It receives the beatific vision only when it is ready for it, when there is no smallest element of self not wholly made perfect, when it can bear that supreme gift of God. Yet we know our prayers can help it. God, for our sakes by some creative action of His omnipotence, speeds up and intensifies the energies of that soul. He fills it with greater energy in suffering, in desiring, in reaching out to God, that its task may be the sooner done.

When on earth a judge remits a sentence, he leaves the culprit in himself as he was before, for no man can directly change another's conscience. When God remits a sentence, it is not by a mere forensic action. When God declares a man just, innocent, holy, stainless, he *is* just, innocent, holy, stainless. When God says, *Fiat Lux*, there *is* light. So when in answer to our prayers God remits the whole or a

part of the sentence of the Holy Souls, the shackles
of past sin do as a matter of fact fall away from that
soul, its stains are being washed away, the rust of
former faults which tarnished its brightness is removed by the omnipotence of God. The weight that
keeps it down and away from God is lifted, and it
rises towards God with instinctive and irresistible
force.

When a man prays for the souls in purgatory,
though his prayer may not obtain the immediate
total release of any of them, he knows that he directly comforts them in some measure, that he
brightens the twilight of their prison-house, that
someone at least in his innermost being feels the
happy results of his prayer.

It is of faith that our prayers are of avail to the
souls in purgatory, but the exact measure and proportion in which the result of our prayers avails
them, in what way the benefit thereof is allocated to
them, has not been revealed to us. It is obvious from
the fact that the Church authorises and sanctions
prayers and Masses for individual faithful departed,
that such prayers and Masses are of advantage to
the individuals to whom they are applied, but how
great the advantage in each case, we must leave to
God's supernatural Providence.

It is sometimes felt by Catholics that, as the rich

can by the payment of honoraria to priests secure the saying of Mass for themselves and their friends after death, the rich have thereby an undue advantage over the poor.

According to the Gospels, riches are rather a hindrance than a help to eternal salvation, and it is very difficult for a rich man to be saved. If, then, the rich man by the proper disposal of his money after his death can obtain the prayers and the Masses of many, it would still have to be shown that such advantage outweighed the initial disadvantage of the possession of riches.

But the real solution of this question lies elsewhere. Two thoughts must be kept in mind. First, that every Mass or prayer offered up for the soul of one of the faithful departed does indeed benefit that individual soul, but its gracious effect on that soul depends, among other things, on the past life of that soul when on earth. History tells us that Henry VIII left prodigious sums for Masses to be offered for his soul. No doubt many thousand times the Sacrifice was actually offered up for him after his death. If that monarch died repentant and was saved, his soul in purgatory received some relief from each Mass as offered, but it may well have been in the decrees of God's justice that the relief granted on account of all Masses said was less than that given after the soli-

tary Mass at the funeral of a poor person, whose life
had been less sinful than that of that notorious king.

Prayers and Sacrifices offered for the dead are
acts of supplication to the mercy of God. God has
deigned to reveal that He listens to these supplications. He will never break that promise, but He does
not therefore abdicate the sovereign rights of His infinite justice and holiness. It would be sacrilegious
folly to make light of sins on earth because one had
somehow secured the prayers of many, and a multitude of Masses after death. Secondly, we must remember that where no prayer or no Mass whatever
is offered up for some individual soul, owing to some
reason beyond his control in life, that soul need not
necessarily be without relief during his waiting in
purgatory.

Every Mass is said for the living and the dead.
Many Masses are said especially for all the faithful
departed. Endless prayers rise daily from the lips of
the devout for all the faithful departed. God, who
hears this ceaseless pleading, will allocate His divine gifts to the Holy Souls as He chooses. One
humble prayer, one secret desire from the lips of a
man, poor and forgotten, that after death he may
have his share in the supplications of the Church,
may secure unto him more than the costly chantry
built by a rich man with less devotion and love of
God.

(8) INDULGENCES FOR SOULS IN PURGATORY

Another strange but not uncommon error must be noticed. Some people imagine that the hundreds of days of indulgence granted by popes or bishops mean so many days less in purgatory. The days mentioned in indulgences have no reference at all to days in purgatory, but to days of ancient canonical penance. Such remission of temporal punishment (still due for sins, the guilt of which is forgiven, if the contrition for all its genuineness is not as great as it should have been) as would be obtained by performance of the canonical punishment of old, is bestowed on him who gains the indulgence.

If such indulgences are applied to souls in purgatory they change their character. The Church has no jurisdiction in purgatory. No pope or bishop can by an act of authority directly lessen the length of stay in purgatory of anyone. The satisfaction to God, obtained by the performance of the indulgence, can be offered up to His Divine Majesty with the supplication to apply its fruit to a soul in purgatory. It is therefore a pleading, a prayer to the Mercy of God to accept the action performed as an indulgence by the living for a suffering soul in the life beyond.

We know that God will accept it in some way, but the days of canonical punishment do not correspond to the number of days in purgatory. We do not even know whether there are days in purgatory.

Time after death is hardly to be compared with time on earth. We have hardly an idea how time applies at all to disembodied souls. In a sense they have reached the ultimate and unchanging state of those who finished their course. Time, even on earth, is largely subjective—a day is like an hour for those who are in joy, but like a year to those who are in pain—time in the stillness beyond the grave may have nothing commensurate to our present counting. To the Holy Souls possibly, even as unto God, a thousand years may be as one day; or one day as a thousand years.

In the case of a Plenary Indulgence applied to the Holy Souls, this application is also made *per modum suffragii, i.e.,* an offering of the satisfactory value of the indulgence, remitting to the living the whole of their canonical punishment. A Plenary Indulgence would remit to the living the whole of their temporal punishment, if the indulgence be received by the penitent in perfect dispositions, for whosoever after absolution performs the canonical punishments of the Church has both the guilt and the punishment of his sin forgiven. The Church Militant, however, having no direct authority over the faithful departed, can only offer to God by way of pleading and prayer the good works done by the living for the dead. God will hear that prayer in the measure in which it seems good in His eyes. Hence the Church's never-ending solicitude for her children who have passed into the Great Beyond.

(9) CAN THE HOLY SOULS HELP THE LIVING?

It is often asked whether the Holy Souls still take any interest in our lives on earth, whether they still know about us, whether they can help us by their prayers as we help them.

The question is a difficult one. The Blessed in heaven see God face to face, and in His eyes as in a mirror can see what passes on this earth. They are in a perfect state of bliss, and the knowledge of their near and dear ones in this world is therefore not withheld from them. With the souls in purgatory it is different. They do not see God face to face, they are in a state of sorrow and punishment, though it be a loving punishment and they be Holy Souls. The above argument for the knowledge of the Blessed fails us therefore in regard to these latter souls. Not possessing their bodies, they have no direct means of communication with this world of sense. Knowledge therefore about the living can only be bestowed upon them by a special gift of God. Whether God often or even normally bestows this gift upon them, the Church has not decided. Two things, however,

can be urged in its favour: the fact of occasional ap-
paritions of the dead, betraying a knowledge of
earthly affairs, and the fact that the Church allows
private prayers asking the intercessions of the Holy
Souls for the living.

No one is bound by his Catholic faith to believe
any individual ghost story, however edifying, and
there can be no doubt that the sorrowing imagination of the surviving has often conjured up phan-
tasms of the dead, which were mere illusions. On the
other hand, during the two millenniums of Church
history so many stories have come down related by
sane, sober and saintly persons, and cherished by so
many whose orthodoxy, piety and good-sense are
above suspicion, that it seems wilful incredulity to
set them all aside as idle fancies. It seems to show
disrespect to the indwelling of the Holy Ghost in the
Church to suppose that He would allow such per-
sistent, yea, age-long superstition amongst the good
and the wise of the faithful.

Moreover, if in the Old Testament Samuel could
appear to Saul and the high priest Onias pray for
the Maccabees, it is but natural to think that in the
New Testament the Holy Souls have knowledge of
the Church Militant.

Then again, if the Holy Souls knew nothing more
about us, nor could help us in any way, the Church
would hardly allow her children privately to ask for

help from these souls, for this would then be an idle and superstitious practice.

Lastly, such complete severance between the Holy Souls and ourselves in interest and prayer would seem to mar the completeness of the Apostles' Creed: I believe in the Communion of the Saints. There the word "Saints" certainly includes all the faithful who are in a state of grace on earth, and it would appear arbitrary to exclude the Holy Souls, confirmed in grace, in purgatory. On such a supposition their communion with us would be only one-sided and not mutual.

If it be urged that the Holy Souls can merit no longer, whatever they do, it is easy to answer that the Saints in heaven cannot merit either; but this does not take away their intercessory power, which is based not on fresh meritorious acts but on the merits of their earthly life, which is over and gone.

It may be urged that the Holy Souls have their will in complete unison with God's will and therefore cannot ask for some special gift apart from the prayer: "Thy Will be done."

This is true of the Saints in heaven likewise. Their hearts, too, beat in perfect harmony with the Will of God, yet they can ask for individual gifts in praying for the living on earth. God Himself, though in eternal possession of infinite joy and the satisfaction of His divine Will, can will and create individual

finite things: there is therefore no reason why the
Saints or the Holy Souls should not ask for them.

Though there is no Catholic dogma on this whole
matter, nevertheless it is a safe inference from revealed truth which may well satisfy Catholic minds.
If it seems strange that there be no public liturgical
prayer asking for the intercession of the Holy Souls,
if such intercession were possible, we must remember that such absence of public prayer is open to
serious doubt, and that to affirm it is begging the
question. It is quite true that there is no liturgical
prayer to any *individual* soul who is not in the
calendar of the Saints in heaven, but who can guar-
antee that in the numberless expressions such as:
Omnes Sancti et Sanctae Dei, intercedite pro nobis,
the words *Sancti et Sanctae* must always be understood to the exclusion of the Holy Souls? It is obvious and natural that when individuals are singled
out by name, they should only be those who already
see God face to face, but this does not prove that
in collective prayers in public the Church consciously excludes, and wishes her children to exclude, all who have not entered final bliss.

The custom of the faithful to invoke the assistance
of their departed dear ones, even immediately after
death, irrespective of their having left purgatory, if
only their death have been a holy one and they de-

parted in *osculo pacis,* is so widespread and constant that it may well reveal the mind of the Church.

Nothing, therefore, hinders us from believing that, though we may not see, nor perceive them in any way—no more in fact than our own guardian angels—the Holy Souls are allowed by the mercy of God to remain in constant touch with those whom they loved on earth and who are their fellow-saints on the road to heaven.

3. Heaven

We see now through a glass in a dark manner: but then face to face. Now I know in part: but then I shall know even as I am known (I Cor. xiii. 12).

(1) HEAVEN IS A PLACE OF REST AND HAPPINESS

HEAVEN is a place of rest. At present we are beings in progress, we are in a state of evolution, we are developing into some future state from hour to hour; hence some restlessness is unavoidable, even in the most holy. We are on a journey, and we cannot stand still before we have reached the end; a perpetual "forward," as it were, is drummed into our ears, however unconsciously; our very inmost being itself is imperfect and craves for its completion. Then we shall be what theologians call *"in termino";* we are no longer on the way; we are at our final end. There is no more "beyond" for us. Every bud finally becomes the full-grown flower, every seed the full plant, every acorn the complete oak; so likewise, man becomes a perfect man, as God wanted him to

48

be. He has taken a lifetime to develop, to maintain and increase his spiritual life; when he enters heaven he is what he will remain for all eternity, he has reached the full stature of his manhood, he will grow no more. Ages may roll on, and scenes may change, but he will ever be the self-same.

He has reached his ultimate end. God had this from all eternity in His mind when He created him and now he has fulfilled the divine ideal fixed eternally for him; hence he will be eternally at rest, at rest within himself, at rest with all creation, at rest with God, who made him and brought him to his end.

We shall be completely happy. Upon earth we have at most, a few passing moments when we are completely, happily satisfied. We may feel in robust health, all may go well with us, we may have just for the hour—or is it only half an hour or a quarter! —all we may desire; we may be full of enjoyment and so occupied with our pleasure that we do not look beyond. Our happiness may be but a humble one, but, at least as long as it lasts, it is fully satisfying, as long, namely, as we give the future no thought. If we do, immeasurable desires surge up within us. Every unsatisfied desire means pain of a kind, means a craving, means a hunger, means a thirst for something which we do not yet possess.

In heaven we shall enter upon a state of which at

present we have no conception, a state of full and
everlasting enjoyment, a state when it will be impossible to form a wish which is not satisfied. We shall
actually be incapable of wishing for more than we
have. Our happiness of course will not be infinite,
that would be impossible for a finite creature. It
will be limited in itself, the happiness of one Saint
will be greater than that of another; none the less
our happiness will completely satisfy us beyond the
possibility of craving for more. Our little cup of enjoyment will be full, though others may, perchance,
have larger vessels than we, and though there will be
boundless oceans of divine happiness beyond.

We must not, however, imagine heaven as a place
where all sorts of fairy wishes are instantaneously
gratified, as if we were reposing on some magic car-
pet. In heaven no new wishes, no new desires will
ever arise, even for a moment, to make us realize
that we lack something which is not already ours.
Heaven is not a sort of emporium of toys, where, on
the expression of any wish, celestial children are
forthwith supplied from the store of God's bounty.
God's little ones will not be taxing their ingenuity
in finding out novelties for the goodness of God to
realize.

Heaven is not the *possible* enjoyment of anything
we shall be able to think of; it will be the *actual* enjoyment, never ending, of the greatest happiness we

can possess. Not a succession of finite good things will please us during the course of successive ages, but the complete possession, all at once, of the highest, the infinite object of all enjoyment, viz.: God, as far as our capacity for happiness goes.

People on earth have been known, when some sudden great happiness befell them, to burst into tears. Apparently the joy was too much for them, as if they could not hold it, as if it overwhelmed them, and being overcome they felt a happy pain at their inability to contain more. Such, but without any feeling of distress, without any tears or trouble, will be the state of the blessed in heaven. They have widened their heart to the uttermost and God fills it, God the beautiful, God the good, God the mighty, and to their utmost power they hold Him and are supremely happy.

It is even difficult to understand how they can possibly have such additional joys as the pleasure and the company of friends, of their kith and kin, of their fellow saints, the additional joys of the pleasures of sight and hearing and feeling, when they receive their bodies again after the General Resurrection. As a matter of fact they will not strictly be *additional* joys, for the Saints will behold all things within God. They will realise God as the cause of all good created by Him, they will thus see the Creator within every creature, and it is He, who thus lives within the hearts of their fellows and friends. Their goodness is but a reflection of His, whom they love and praise and enjoy.

In this life we are forced to consider creatures for themselves apart from God; though our reason tells us they are but effects of God's goodness, manifestations of His beauty and power. Then we shall actually, directly perceive that all created goodness exists only in virtue of being a reflection of His glory. Our love for our friends shall only be a mode of our enjoyment of God Himself.

(2) THE MEANING OF THE BEATIFIC VISION

At present, when we grasp or understand something outside ourselves, we do so by *species intelligibiles,* as the Scholastics say. This might be translated: "thought-images," or rather *ideas,* for thought in itself is really imageless. The thing outside us is first brought as it were within us, through the senses. These senses, being affected, produce a phantasm, a picture, on the brain, or rather on the purely material animal imagination. Such sense-images we have in common with the mere animal creation, with the beasts, the birds, and the fishes. In men, however, possessed of intellect, these sense-images are grasped by the mind, and in grasping them, the human intelligence becomes in some way

modified or impressed. Not that the mind is purely
passive; on the contrary the intelligence grasps the
image, strips it of all concrete and individual notes,
lets it sink into the womb of the mind and thus con-
ceives it and brings it forth. Hence the term *concept,*
an idea conceived in the mind.

If it be allowable to compare material things with
spiritual ones, one might compare it to a seal
stamped on soft wax—only with this difference: that
we think of the metal seal as the hard substance
forcing itself on the soft wax, the seal being the
active, the wax the passive part so to speak. In our
mind, however, it is our intelligence which plays the
active part, it grasps the sense-image, as if the hot
and flowing wax by its own energy fused itself round
the seal. Thus the thing outside comes within our intelligence by an intellectual process, viz., the forming of the *idea.*

This *idea* we can consider from a twofold aspect.
First, as an impression to which the mind in a sense
is passive. The mind's activity is conditioned and
limited precisely by the sense-image which it grasps.
We can consider it, secondly, as an expression, or a
species expressa, as the Schoolmen say, an expressed
image, a thought-equivalent of the thing outside.
The thing outside, however, as it is in itself, must
ever remain outside the mind. The substance, the
inner reality of external objects, the very essence of

the outside world we cannot really take within our understanding; we must always use these *ideas* or *species intelligibiles* as intermediaries between ourselves and outer reality.

Such is the make of our mind, we cannot think in any other fashion while we are here upon earth. But the way in which we shall know God will be quite different. First, of course, there will be no sense-image, for God is in no sense whatever material. All our notions here on earth are abstracted from sense-data; however refined and spiritual, none the less, nothing can at present be in our mind which is not somehow connected and ultimately derived from what our senses told us; our only avenue to reality lies here on earth by the road of the senses. Our mind indeed is purely spiritual, but the only data on which it can exercise its spiritual powers are data obtained in the first instance from the senses. After life, however, we shall, by a wonder of God's omnipotence, directly and without intermediary see God, and in so doing we shall dispense with any sense-data whatever. How this is possible we cannot understand, but it shall be so. Hence we shall in no sense imagine God, but only know Him with our intelligence; there will be nothing to imagine but only God Himself to understand.

Moreover, there will not even be a pure mental representation as an intermediary between us and

God. Such representation, if it existed, would be something created, something finite and limited, something after all less than God, and we would then know not God Himself as He is in Himself, but only our own created thought-picture of Him.

Hence again, by a wonder of God's omnipotence, God shall come into immediate contact with our mind, with nothing whatever between us and Him. It is not correct to say that we shall see God in the sense of merely looking at Him. One only looks *at* an outside object, and as long as it remains an outside object, one can only reach it by the means of, by the lens—as it were—of our idea or concept. However clear the crystal of that lens, however sharp the picture thrown, it would always remain only a picture. But in seeing God hereafter there will be no picture whatsoever. No mental representation of God could ever make us eternally happy but only God Himself.

(3) OUR INTIMACY WITH GOD

God's intimacy with us will be so great that He will be in no sense outside us at all, but within us; we shall grasp His very being within the very powers of our mind. On earth we have no experience of such a kind of knowledge, we have never as yet known anything after this fashion. We have never really known the substance of anything, we have only known things by their manifestations, we had always to leave the things themselves outside and through the go-betweens of sense and thought-images reach them by an intricate process of thinking.

The only mode of knowing of which we have experience and which comes closer to our future mode of knowing God, is the way in which we know ourselves. We are most intimately present to ourselves, we know ourselves because we are ourselves. Still, even here, though there is some direct contact between the knower and the known, it is most imperfect. Though we seem aware of our own existence by the fact that we are ourselves, for everything else we have laboriously to gather material to understand our own inmost being, and most people have a lamentably faint and incorrect idea of what they themselves are.

On earth, however, this is the nearest approach to immediate knowledge, and hence the Scriptures say that "then we shall know even as we are known."

Now when we say that God shall be within us, we must of course set aside all notions of local place and habitation. It has nothing to do with place, or space or extension, or measurement of any kind. It is no local nearness, it is something much more intimate than that. It shall be life within life, being within being. Put a bar of iron in a blazing furnace, till it is white-hot, till the eye can no longer distinguish between it and the surrounding fire, still that metal shall always be less pervaded by the fire than the soul is pervaded by God.

Now as a matter of fact, already here on earth we are pervaded by God; in Him we live, we move, we have our being, but we do not realise it. Then we shall be fully aware of God within us. How shall this divine consciousness of God be brought about? In the only way in which it can be. We shall be like unto Him. Our life shall vibrate in unison with His and we shall know it. We shall indeed always remain distinct from Him, we shall never lose our separate identity, we shall never lose our individual consciousness. He and we shall never fuse into one being, He shall ever be God and we His creatures; but if we cling to that fundamental truth, we can never exaggerate the intimacy and closeness of our union with Him.

A somewhat childish, yet, perchance, helpful, comparison would be that of the filament in an electric lamp. The current passes through it, it becomes light-giving, and heat-bearing, it is commonly described as "alive" by electricity; its inmost being is in a state of intense activity corresponding to the immense store of energy within the dynamo; the innermost recesses of its substance are stimulated by an irresistible force which transmutes and transforms its very self. Thus our souls shall become carriers of the divine life-current of God. In a sense we ourselves shall become light and life. "In Thy light we shall see the light."

(4) THE GIFT OF THE *Lumen Gloriæ*

Were it not that God created within us a capacity to receive Him, see Him and possess Him, our being would never be able to support His Presence. This gift, enabling us to bear God, the Schoolmen call *lumen gloriæ*. This gift is so great that it not only exceeds our human needs or rights or powers, but those of any possible creature whatsoever. None of the Cherubim so mighty, none of the Seraphim so holy, that such a gift would be natural to him. It is as far above their powers as it is above ours.

Though God can bestow it on creatures as a free gift from His infinite bounty, yet even He could not make a creature that would find this power within the normal range of its nature. For it is indeed God's own life communicated.

Man is tempted to think of such a communication as beyond what is metaphysically possible. How can a finite creature with finite powers of knowledge know the infinite God? How with finite powers of will and enjoyment can he possess the infinite divine goodness and beauty? How can the limited encompass the Unlimited? Is all this not a contradiction in terms and a denial of logic and reason? Is it not like a square circle, or parallel lines that are supposed to meet?

It is indeed with the dogma of the Beatific Vision as with the dogma of the Blessed Trinity or the Incarnation. At first glance they seem to assert the impossible, and alas, impatient minds forthwith set them aside as unthinkable and contrary to reason. But on second thoughts more docile minds realise that, though above reason, no dogma is against it.

If the Catholic Church taught that, in the Beatific Vision, the human mind encompassed the infinite God and that it fathomed the very depths of the Godhead, then she would assert, not a mystery, but an impossibility. But she does not do so. She teaches that the souls in heaven apprehend God, but not that they comprehend Him. Human intelligence shall grasp Him, but not embrace Him. No finite power can encompass the infinite. In the Beatific Vision the mind of man shall be in direct contact with God as the Object of its understanding; we shall be in immediate intelligent touch with God, but our act of intelligence shall always be, and cannot but be, the act of a creature and therefore limited and finite. How an Infinite Being can come into direct contact with a finite understanding, that is a mystery, a mystery at present utterly beyond our power of conception, but it is not an impossibility.

It is a mystery in the supernatural order somewhat analogous to the natural mystery of our creation. By our very existence we are the limited finite results of the infinite power and wisdom of God. We only exist because we are known and willed by God. His knowledge and will is the very intrinsic ground and reason of our being. God's knowledge and will is always infinite, and yet we are but finite. How can this be? We do not understand, we only know that God is and that we are. The fact is indisputable, but we cannot explain it. So likewise it is a fact, revealed by God, that the Blessed in heaven see Him face to face. How this can be we cannot explain, we only know that it is so.

God, then, remains unfathomable even to the greatest of His saints. They see Him, but none can see to the very depths of His divine being. God is a world, a wide universe, which none of the Blessed has ever totally explored. Even after millions of cycles of ages, neither Mary, the Queen of heaven, nor Michael, the Prince of the heavenly host, shall exhaust the greatness of the divine Majesty. It is an ocean on which the little craft of created intelligences can forever press forward in all directions, for it is a sea without a shore. As a pretty, many-coloured insect on swift wings floats on the summer breeze and allows itself to be driven along in the seemingly boundless air; as a lark rises in the apparently boundless sky, so do the Blessed roam about in the limitless wideness of God.

(5) THE NEVER-ENDING FRESHNESS OF HEAVEN

Bishop Hedley has somewhere a telling comparison. He speaks of a little child let free for the first time in a great field to pick flowers. It sees hundreds and thousands at the time, the one prettier than the other; it is bewildered by the plenty of loveliness surrounding it, but the boundaries of the field it does not see. Thus shall be the Child of God, who, after death, is allowed to gaze on the limitless expanse of the beauty of God. It cannot go beyond the blissful surprise of the first moments of its glory.

Sometimes on earth, at the unveiling of something very beautiful, people have caught their breath in intense and happy amazement at the sight granted to them, but such keen moments of deep joy and astonishment are very short. A second glance is less powerful than the first, and at the third we possess ourselves again. It will not be so when we see God. At the first unveiling of God's beauty we shall stand spellbound, and even eternity shall never break the spell. The novelty shall never wear away. The freshness of His glory shall never pass. God, so old, shall always be new. St. John, in the Apocalypse, describes God as saying, "Behold, I make all things new." These words express a profounder meaning than the ordinary reader is apt to gather. God makes all things new, and no sequence of centuries shall ever make them old.

Herein, no doubt, lies the secret that heaven, though everlasting, shall never grow stale, never pall upon its citizens or fill them with weariness. It stands written in the Psalmist: "The heavens declare the glory of God, day unto day uttereth speech and night unto night showeth knowledge." This has been applied, not merely to the wonders of the material firmament and the glories of the starry skies, but to the heaven of God's unveiled glory above. During the long length of eternity one day utters unto the other the news of the fresh wonders seen in the Godhead, and the Blessed to one another set forth the story of the ever new and strange sights which have met their adoring eyes.

How this can be is not easy to understand, for the mind of the Blessed has reached its utmost development and is already filled with divine knowledge to the utmost of its capacity. In one sense it can no longer increase in wisdom; it is no longer on the way towards perfection; it has arrived at the perfect state, when mind and will, energising to the utmost, hold already all they can possibly contain.

The mind, then, of the Blessed is under one aspect stationary and not progressive. Only imperfect things can make progress. Nevertheless, God, leaving the power of their mind unchanged and keeping Himself always as the Object of their knowledge, can, being infinite, remain new to them and work on their mind what, according to our present earthly way of thinking, would be equivalent to variation and everlasting novelty.

(6) OUR PERSONAL FRIENDSHIP WITH GOD

We have hitherto spoken of God as an Object of Knowledge, almost as if He were an infinite *thing*. We have spoken of Being, of Life, of Light, of Majesty and so on, which more or less suggest something impersonal, something unspeakably beautiful, but with the still objectivity of a tableau. This, however, is only due to the poverty of our language, which can express but very partially the grandeur of God. We must recall to our mind that what we shall behold is an individual, personal Spirit. We shall come into contact with a person, not with a thing, or rather we shall see Three Persons, the Father, the Son, and the Holy Ghost.

Our intimacy with God will be one of personal intercourse, one of personal friendship. It will be truly mutual and reciprocal affection. If we think

that our union with God will be too exalted, too
magnificent, to allow of such a humble and com-
monplace description as mutual friendship, we are
mistaken.

On earth, friendship implies some equality of sta-
tion and position in life. The learned do not associate with the unlettered, the very rich with the very
poor, the refined with those who are boorish. In
friendship amongst men the party that has the
higher gifts is ever afraid to demean himself by ac-
cepting as friend one of lesser degree, as the humbler
partner is likely to give to his intimacy a lower tone
and character. Where two friends are men of greatly
different acquirements or privileges, there will in-
evitably be conscious and perceptible condescension
from one to another. Condescension is rooted in a
dread to lose dignity, a dignity insecurely held, a
dignity limited in extent.

The infinite God has no such dread, hence there
is no condescension which would kill friendship.
Moreover, between God and the Blessed there never
can be any comparison; He is the Creator and they
are His creatures. The *lumen gloriæ* by which they
are lifted up to a life similar to His is His own free
gift and creation. There is no cold condescension between the Maker and the thing He has made. There
is no need of an effort to make a show of superiority
towards one's own handiwork. Hence God can em-

brace His creature with infinite abandonment of love, and the creature can respond to the utmost of its capacity. Mutual friendship can thus arise between God and man in the truest and strictest sense of the word.

(7) GOD THE FATHER, THE SON AND THE HOLY GHOST

Therefore, a friendship exists between the Blessed on one hand and God the Father, the Son and the Holy Ghost on the other; an adoring friendship on their side, an infinitely loving one on His.

The divine Paternity of God the Father will encompass those who have obeyed the voice of His Son: "Come, ye blessed of My Father, and receive the kingdom prepared for you from the beginning of the world." God's adopted children will eternally give their hearts to the Father that made them. This divine adoption is not a mere legal fiction, as adoption must necessarily be here on earth, but a reality produced by the omnipotence of God. It is an objective similarity, a real likeness between the children of adoption and the Only Begotten One. The Blessed have entered into their Father's house, not locally, but by a community of life. He has lifted them up so that they are able to share His glory and inherit His kingdom. By the *lumen gloriæ* He has made them able to understand His ideals, His ways,

and He has removed the natural incongruity of men
consorting with God. He has taught them to say to
Him what Christ said: "Abba, Father!" He has
taught them the speech of God and they can hold
sweet converse with their Father.

The Blessed in heaven know God the Son, their
Redeemer, the Word of God and the splendour of
His Glory. They understand how He is eternally
being born of His Father, God of God, light of light,
true God of true God, consubstantial with the
Father, through whom all things are made. The
meaning of the words in the Creed is faint and
difficult to us now. We hold them by sheer faith and
they remain obscure. Then the sight of that mystery,
but mystery no longer, will throw us into transports
of joy. We shall recognize the Eternal Word as
God and as eternally distinct from the Father, and
another Person.

That Other Person we shall love as the One who
took our human nature for our sakes and became
man. That Other Person shall love us, for He is by
nature what we are by grace, and our very adoption
consists in being like unto Him. In a sense beyond
our present power to grasp, there shall be a brother-
hood between us and the Only begotten Son of God.

The Blessed in heaven shall know God the Holy
Ghost, the personal, subsisting Love, who proceed-
eth from the Father and the Son, who together with

them is adored and glorified. The indwelling of that Spirit within us through grace is now a matter of faith; then it will be the very life of our life consciously perceived and possessed. The breathing forth of the Holy Ghost from the Father and the Son, instead of being a dark mystery, shall be as the effulgence of the sun at noonday. The Blessed shall be illumined and warmed by His divine going-forth to fill the boundless greatness of the Triune God.

It shall be for all a Whitsuntide that will last for ever. Without the flames and parted tongues as it were of fire, visible over the heads of all, the Blessed shall be filled to overflowing with an inward Presence giving them joy, power and understanding till they proclaim to all creation the greatness of God. All shall know themselves temples of the Holy Ghost, and all shall lovingly adore the Holy One, who dwells within.

The threefold "Holy, Holy, Holy, Lord God of Hosts" shall not be sung towards some distant throne of fearsome Majesty, but shall be the affectionate worship of a God close at hand, the love of a divine friend within.

The Beatific Vision then shall be the essence of our eternal happiness; to know and love God as He is means a sea of happiness the shores of which we shall never reach.

(8) THE SACRED HUMANITY OF CHRIST

In God, moreover, we shall see the Sacred
Humanity of Christ. God is man, even as we,
throughout eternity. When on Mount Thabor at the
Transfiguration, Peter, James and John saw Christ
for a moment with His face as the sun and His garments white as snow, they were beyond themselves
in amazement and wished to set up tents that they
might remain on the blissful mountain for ever. Yet
then Christ's humanity was translucent to but one
ray of the divine glory, as much as their mortal eyes
could bear. In heaven that Human Nature, united
in one person to God the Son, shall show forth the
glory of God, for in Christ—as the Scriptures say—
dwelleth the Godhead bodily.

No one has ever read the Gospels devoutly without feeling the irresistible attraction of the Man
from Nazareth. Many have spent a lifetime in study-
ing the features of the Fairest of men. No Christian
but has dreamt sometimes of the lovableness of the
Babe of Bethlehem, the Boy at Nazareth, the
Prophet in Galilee, the Lover of children, the Friend
of the home at Bethany, the Sufferer at Gethsemane,
the willing Victim on the Cross of Calvary, the
Risen One who called Mary by her name on Easter
morn. Few have not felt rising to their lips the cry of

the Magdalene near the Sepulchre: "Rabboni! O my Master," or the cry of Thomas: "My Lord and my God!" Few would not repeat with Peter: "Master, who knowest all things, Thou knowest that I love Thee."

In heaven this Jesus will be the companion of the Blessed, not merely a gracious monarch on His throne, worshipped from a distance, but the close and loving friend of each and all.

The Incarnation is not something over and gone, it is an eternal reality. The Incarnation is not merely a scheme of God, devised for our redemption, a something that had its value in the past, and which was needed that God-made-man might atone for our sins. The Incarnation is not merely a help during the span of our earthly life; it is eternally the central fact of all creation, and all that is, is ranged round and radiates from Jesus Our Lord. He shall still be the centre of our life during our eternal joys, for He is not someone distinct from God; He is God the Son in our human nature. His companionship will be the delight of the Saints.

We shall not merely acclaim Him on state occasions as our King and Lord, happy if with royal gesture He notices us for an instant amongst the multitude of Blessed; each one of us shall have Him as our personal friend. How this shall be, we cannot now explain, but it is surely not impossible to Him

who, during our mortal life, gives Himself whole and
entire, with Godhead and manhood, soul and body,
flesh and blood to each communicant amongst ten
thousand.

Thus through never-ending ages He will be to
each one of us a friend, who sticks closer than a
brother. Our love for Him, and His love for us, shall
bring home to us incessantly the joys of the Beatific
Vision.

In Galilee, five thousand people could follow Him
into the desert, forgetful of fatigue and heedless of
hunger and thirst, overcome by the sacred fascina-
tion of His Presence till they were in danger of faint-
ing by the way. This was but a foreshadowing of a
greater spiritual reality in the land of the Saints,
where the multitudes of men and women will be
swayed by the divine charm of the Man who is God
Incarnate, nor will they ever be in peril of fatigue or
hunger or thirst, for they have eaten of the tree of
life, the food of immortality.

(9) OUR KNOWLEDGE OF OUR FRIENDS IN HEAVEN

One of the commonest questions asked by Christians, who give some thought to the life hereafter, is
this: "Shall we know one another in heaven?" It is
to be feared that in many instances the question be-
trays but faint understanding of what the essential

joys of heaven are, for the happiness of heaven is essentially the sight of God and not the company of creatures. Still the question is natural, considering that the keenest enjoyment we know of in the natural order is that of the love of our fellow men, and that the separation of those near and dear to us now, would seem to lessen and mar even the joys of heaven.

Our fear, however, is totally unfounded. The Revelation of St. John, in which the heavenly Jerusalem is pictured under the symbolism of an earthly city, describes for us the Blessed as evidently in intercourse with one another. Moreover, our very reason indicates that God, who makes us eternally happy as men, will not without rhyme or reason, deprive us of those joys which are connatural to our manhood.

There is danger that in the popular mind, the occupation of the Blessed in heaven is viewed as something constrained and unnatural. It is imagined as a perpetual psalmody and recital of prayers, accompanied by incessant peals of music. The Saints are imagined as members of a choir that never disbands. Alas, to some simple souls it seems as if going to heaven would mean to be for ever in church, and in church one is not supposed to take notice of another; to look around is a fault, to speak to one's neighbour a sin.

Our conduct in church is conditioned by the fact that in this world it is exceedingly difficult to fix our mind on God, and for the short hour that we happen to be in church we had better make the uttermost effort to keep God before our eyes. Owing to our present frailty, this is irreconcilable with intercourse with our neighbour.

In heaven, things are different. In heaven we are not tempted to forget God, and nothing whatever can draw our attention away from Him. He is the very breath of our life, and no one forgets to breathe even when conversing with friends. We shall see God in all creatures. A humble comparison may help our imagination. When we have looked for a while in a strong light and then fix our eyes on the objects around us, the little circle or disc of light seems to follow wherever we look; in fact we see all things through it as in a luminous haze; so, once in heaven, we shall see all things in the light of God, and there is no danger of their averting us from God.

Yes, we shall know our friends in heaven, and we shall know them better than we ever understood them on this earth. Here, our understanding of one another is very imperfect. Which friend is not often baffled by the behaviour of a friend, however much he may like him? Who is there who is so fortunate

that he can claim to have a friend who never misunderstood him?

Even in the measure in which we understand one
another, there are so many shortcomings, foibles and
faults which we would rather not understand. In
heaven there is no danger in knowing one another
through and through, for every one of the Saints is
confirmed in sanctity; there is no spot or stain, no
secret weakness in the life of any. Friendships on
earth are often unsteady, whimsical and disappoint-
ing; such is not the love amongst the Saints.

Nor, on the other hand, need we dread that love
in heaven will be based so exclusively on degrees of
sanctity, so measured by a sense of duty, so re-
strained by the requirements of holiness, that friendship will lose all that we now understand by natural
affection for kith and kin. Not so does the Catholic
faith teach us the mysteries of heaven. Devout imagination has filled heaven with the love of God for
Mary, who is the Mother of God the Son. If Christ
has not lost the love for the Mother that bore Him,
how should the Blessed lose their love for those who
were near and dear to them on earth?

No doubt the natural love for parents and kindred
will be spiritualised, but it will certainly not be
destroyed. In heaven we shall be supernatural, not
unnatural. He that has decreed the resurrection of

the body certainly wishes us eternally to lead natural human lives, glorified and exalted indeed, but not changed into something inhuman and alien to the instincts He Himself has instilled in our breasts.

(10) OUR INTERCOURSE WITH MARY, SAINTS AND ANGELS

In heaven, then, we shall have numberless friends, not merely our relatives and former friends on earth, but, in a sense, that whole vast multitude which no one can number, who are our companions for ever. First and foremost, the Virgin Mother of Christ, who received us all as children under the Cross of her son, and who will gladly take us under the wide mantle of her glory on the steps of the throne of her Son. Those who, during their mortal life, have learnt ever to join together the names of Jesus and Mary shall not learn to separate them in eternity.

After the Queen of heaven, comes the whole army of the Saints of God, Apostles and martyrs, confessors and virgins—that vast array of men and women, who have reached their final end even as we, who are God's children not less than we. How we shall first strike acquaintance with our favourite heroes and heroines of God, with those whose names were household words on our lips during our sojourn in this vale of tears, of that we can at present dream a great deal but know very little for certain.

If we think their number too great ever to become intimate with us, let us not forget that we shall have an eternity in which to form our friendships, and that the heavenly city will be an easy meeting place even for those who during their earthly days were far apart in many ways. It is said that friendships spontaneously arise between those who have a friend in common: if that be so, no lengthy introduction is needed between those who have a bosom friend in common in Jesus, the Lover of men.

The Angelic Host, though different from us in nature, is not beyond the sphere of the love of the children of men. They are elder brethren, but brethren none the less. What intercourse is possible between the Seraphim, the Cherubim and ourselves, at present passes our imagination. Yet the angels must be closely akin to us, for otherwise God would not have used them as our guardians, and Gabriel and his fellows would not have been messengers chosen to bring good tidings to men; Raphael could not have walked with Tobias on his journey, and Michael would not have been Prince of the people of God.

It is an old belief that we men shall occupy the thrones left vacant in heaven by the fall of Lucifer and his followers, when the ancient Dragon in his fall tore away one-third of the stars of heaven. If such be the truth, the human race will not be a race of intruders into the realm of God, but welcomed and beloved by those who never fell away from their place of light in the beginning. We shall move amongst the principalities and powers, the angels and archangels with ease, for we shall possess the freedom of the Eternal City above.

(11) OUR DIGNITY AND SECURITY IN HEAVEN

The New Testament loves to describe our future happiness as the possession of a Kingdom: "Receive the Kingdom" is Christ's invitation to enter everlasting life. This expression is no doubt chosen by the Holy Ghost to convey the Royal Estate and Sovereign dignity of the Blessed, which is the outcome both of their inward holiness and of the sense of power and dominion over creation which God bestows upon them.

The Blessed have shaken themselves free from every bond of subjection, they have an inward sense of liberty and spontaneity, of untramelled choice of all that is good, of mastery over themselves and mastery over all creatures, for they know that God has worked all things for the sake of the elect. They have, indeed, inherited a kingdom in which none will refuse homage to their sanctity, none resist their wishes, in which their will is law, for their will is never out of harmony with the omnipotent will of God.

The Scriptures lay much stress on the symbolism of crown and sceptre and robes and thrones. This symbolism indicates the effulgence of the sanctity of the Saints, the nobility of their innermost selves, the triumphant power of their blessed will, the lofty height of their mighty thoughts and the security of their changeless happiness, which is as a diadem on their brow.

Their supreme security will be an incessant all-pervading blissful thought, which will act as a refreshing fragrance amid the joys of heaven. To have and to hold whatever they possess, in absolute permanency of tenure, without even a passing shadow of uncertainty, is a characteristic of the estate of the Blessed. In them the most intense activity and ceaseless energy is combined with complete tranquillity and inward peace.

The Schoolmen speak of God as "pure act," for in Him there is no potentiality whatever, but this pure activity co-exists with the stillness of His immutable Will. No created being can thus combine complete unchangeableness with continuous energy, but the higher in the scale of being and the nearer to God, the closer the approach to God's way of life.

Thus the Saints will combine, each in his own degree, the peace of immovable being with the busy

stir of spontaneous and forceful life. To think of the
Saints as peaceful contemplatives of the holiness of
God, however true, is inadequate, for it does not
sufficiently call up before our mind the throbbing
energy of their inward life. This world is dull and
slow and sluggish compared with the brilliant activi-
ties of the humblest of the Saints. Their days with
God are crowded days, though the fever of haste is
far away.

It is difficult, in fact, quite to understand how far
the sequence of time shall still apply to those who
have come to their final end. Time is a measurement
of duration. For God there is no time. He never
began and He will never end, hence to Him no
measurement applies. For Him there is no past or
future, but only the present. To have lost the past
and to have to wait for the future is an imperfection
impossible to Him, who possesses the whole of His
infinite being all at once. The divine, timeless eternity of God can never be completely the lot of the
Saints, for though they shall never end, still they
have known a beginning; they are but creatures, not
God.

On the other hand, having entered into a changeless state, having obtained the full completion of
their being, having arrived at that stage to which
there is no beyond, time will certainly apply to them
in a different way than it applies to us now. Even

now, an hour's keen pleasure passes quickly, an hour's pain is incredibly long. Were it not that we have learnt mechanically to divide our time by the space between sunrise and sunset, or other material or seasonal changes around us, by the fewness of years between birth and death, our time would be almost purely subjective.

How we shall measure life hereafter—if we do measure it—we cannot know in this life. Perhaps it will be true to us, as it is true of God: "a thousand years are as one day."

4. The General Judgment

IF THE SOUL be judged forthwith after death, what further need is there for a General Judgment? In what do they differ? The General Judgment follows the resurrection of the body. Then men shall be judged as men, when body and soul shall be again united. It is meet and just that previous to the entry of the host of the redeemed into the eternal celestial city, where in the full completion of their manhood they shall abide for ever, there should be an open display of the whole human race to vindicate the justice of the ways of God and the triumph of Christ, who came to redeem them. It seems natural that risen man should forthwith stand before the Judgment Seat of Him that made him. Human eyes and ears should hear the sentence, and the human race gathered together should acclaim the Divine decree that will settle all things.

It is meet and just that Christ, who came in lowliness in the days of Bethlehem, and who was raised on Golgotha on the Cross of shame, should revisit the earth in great power and majesty coming on the clouds of heaven. It is right that the scene of His sorrows should be the scene of His triumph. It is right that the just, who passed their years forgotten and despised, should be invested with glory in the sight of those who once prospered in their wickedness and trampled under foot the poor and the meek.

The world's history is like a tapestry the pattern of which is only seen on one side, the other side shows only incongruous lines and colours. Until the last day God's tapestry is not quite woven and its design not quite completed. Only the obverse has been shown, and its right and true side we have only been able to guess. Then shall all men see God's age-long plan fulfilled and the world's history shall make manifest the wisdom, the power, the goodness, the holiness of God.

Then all men, the lost as well as the saved, shall be assembled to bear witness that it is well done.

Every conscience and every secret motive shall lie bare for all to see, that all may recognize that God is a righteous Judge and gives to everyone according to his works. The tortuous ways of the wicked shall be exposed, and the simplicity of the just no longer despised. The long-suffering grace of God that strove with sinners and that beckoned them to repentance, shall be seen, and the deliberate perversity of their will which set aside the solicitations of the kindness of God. The might of God's grace shall be shown in the hearts of the just, how it triumphed notwithstanding their frailty and brought them to that moment of victory. Then all things from the day when the First Two stood in Eden, to that last and final day when myriads stand before the Son of Man to receive the award from His lips, which can never be reversed—all things will be woven together by God into a crown of glory and an effulgence of His divine goodness. Then even the damned will have their share in making manifest the triumph of good over evil and the superabundance of the bounty of God.

It is of faith that Christ in His human nature will return to judge the living and the dead. Christ testified to this truth before Caiphas the high priest: "You shall see the Son of Man sitting at the right hand of the power of God and coming on the clouds of heaven." The Angels on Ascension Day told the Apostles: "This Jesus whom you have seen go up into heaven, shall so come again as you have seen Him ascend unto heaven." This truth the Apostles preached to the first converts in Palestine and St. Peter claimed: "He (Christ) charged us to preach unto the peoples and to give testimony that it is He who is ordained of God to be the Judge of the living and the dead." It was Christ Himself who had in detail explained this to His Apostles: "The Father judgeth not any man, but He hath given all judgment unto the Son that all may honour the Son even as they honour the Father. Amen, amen, I say unto you the hour cometh and now is, when the dead shall hear the voice of the Son of God. . . . Marvel not at this, for the hour cometh that all that are in the tombs shall hear His voice and shall come forth; they that have done good unto the resurrection of life; and they that have done ill unto the resurrection of judgment."

In carrying out the preparation for His judgment, Christ shall use the ministry of angels: He shall send His angels to gather His elect from the four winds, from the uttermost bounds of the earth. The "trumpet of the angel" may be but a metaphor of speech, but it must be a metaphor for a great reality: the sudden irresistibly compelling force of the angelic host bringing all men together. People do often wish to know where on earth the judgment is to take place. Some have mentioned the valley of Jehoshaphat, spoken of in the prophet Joel. This valley, however, is but a symbolic designation of the place of judgment wherever it shall be. Jehoshaphat is but the Hebrew for "Jehovah judges." The numbers of all men that shall have existed and exist at the Last Day will be so great that no valley on earth would be large enough for them, even if they stood shoulder to shoulder. Moreover, according to St. Paul, we shall at the resurrection be carried up towards

Christ into the clouds. If in such a matter a guess be
allowed, we may imagine that the judgment will indeed be somewhere on earth, but risen bodies are
not subject to laws of earthly gravity and they may
therefore rise as in a vast amphitheatre, encircling
the throne of the Judge placed in the height of the
heavens.

It is clear from the Scriptures that the evil angels
shall in some way be present at this Judgment. We
read: "The angels that kept not their principality,
but left their proper habitations, God kept in everlasting bonds under darkness unto the judgment of
the great day." It is therefore meant as a spectacle
for the whole of God's intelligent creation.

Christ has revealed that as He has deigned to associate the Apostles with Himself in the founding
and spreading of His kingdom on earth, so shall He
associate the Apostles with Himself on the Day of
Judgment. This is indicated by His promise that they
"will sit on twelve thrones to judge" the elect. St.
John in his Revelation gives us a description which
though obviously metaphorical is the greatest and
most sublime account which God has deigned to
leave us. With the exception of the celestial appear-
ance of the Cross on which Christ died, the triumphant display of which tradition foretells, the Church
has not dared to add to this inspired vision, and it is
best to leave the reader with a quotation of its

words: "I saw a great white throne and Him that sat upon it. The earth and the heaven fled away from His face and they were found no more. I saw the dead, the great and small, standing before the throne, and books were opened: and another book was opened, which is the book of life: and the dead were judged out of the things which were written in the books, according to their works. And the sea gave up the dead that were therein and death and the netherworld gave up the dead that were in them: and they were judged every man according to their works. Death and the netherworld were cast into the lake of fire. And if anyone was not found written in the book of life, he was cast into the lake of fire. And I saw a new heaven and a new earth: for the first heaven and the first earth had passed away."

5. The Resurrection of the Body

THERE exists a widespread error amongst non-Catholic Christians with regard to the state of the departed previous to the Second Coming of Christ and the General Resurrection. It is thought that these disembodied souls exist in a certain trance or sleep, from which they will be awakened by the trumpet call of the Last Day. The General Resurrection is considered, not as a rising of the body merely, but a rising of the soul, as if the soul during the interval between death and Judgment Day were deprived of all, or nearly all, its powers and without the vision of God, or at most like the souls in the Limbo of the ancient patriarchs. This strange idea is not quite new, for it occurs in some early Greek writers, and has long found favour amongst the "Orthodox" in the East, but the Catholic Church emphatically rejects it.

(1) THE REALITY OF OUR RISEN BODY

According to Catholic teaching, death is immediately followed by the private or individual judgment, upon which immediately follows heaven, hell or purgatory. In any of these three states, the soul is in the full possession of its powers, with the sole exception of those which relate to the body, because its body is given to corruption in the grave. The souls in heaven, though without the body, possess the Beatific Vision, which is the very essence of their eternal happiness, and they only wait for those lesser joys which will come from the reunion with their body. Manichæans and Gnostics in early days rejected the resurrection of the body, because they held the flesh to be a principle of evil. This led to the Church's emphasis on this doctrine and the insertion of the words in the Apostolic Creed. In this Creed, as in many others, the words used are, not the resurrection of the dead, which might conceivably be misunderstood, but *"resurrectio carnis"*—"the resurrection of the flesh," which left no loophole for misunderstanding.

This doctrine the Church has most sedulously guarded. First, by condemning the speculations of Origenism that the risen body of Christ and that of the Saints after the last day, was "ætherial," a sort of globular, lightsome cloud, or that at the end of the ages, Christ and the Saints would shed their material bodies and then only "Mind" would remain.

Secondly, by asserting again and again, that the body in which we shall rise, will be the identical

body in which we now live and none other. We shall
rise, not merely in *a* body, but in *our* body.

Beyond, however, asserting the identity of the
body in heaven and the body on earth, the Church
has not gone. Now it is a matter of controversy in
what the identity of a body precisely consists. Science
tells us that our bodies continually change. An adult
has apparently changed the particles which have
made up his body as an infant, very many times,
when he has reached middle age. The old man who
totters into the grave has the identical body he had
when, as a newborn babe, he slept in his cradle. But
few things are more certain than that no atom of
matter at all, or at most an infinitesimally small
quantity, remains from birth to death. The human
body we realise to be in continual flux like a flowing
stream, the bed of which remains, but the water of
which ever passes on. What constitutes the principle
of its identity we may leave to philosophers to dis-
cuss. Sufficient has been said to show that the gibes
sometimes cast at the doctrine of the sameness of
the human body in the resurrection are misplaced in
men who do not even know how to explain the
sameness of the human body during life.

When Christ rose from the dead, He raised the
same matter to life which had once constituted His
living body. This matter had been guarded by the
omnipotence of God from all corruption. Nay,

more, we are taught that the Personality of God the
Son, the Second Person of the Blessed Trinity, remained hypostatically united to the lifeless form
which Joseph of Arimathea and Nicodemus buried
on Good Friday and which remained lifeless till
Easter morn. When Christ was taken from the
Cross, the body taken down was not merely one
that had once been the body of the Son of God,
but it was continuing to be *His* body, for its very
existence was bound up with His own Personality;
it remained the human body of God.

With us matters are different. Our bodies shall
be given to the corruption of the grave, turned to
ashes and be mingled with the common dust of the
earth. Moreover, we possess no personality apart
from, or independent of, our soul; hence at death
our connection with the matter which was once our
body ceases. It is, therefore, not conclusive to argue
that because Christ reassumed the same matter as
His body, we at our resurrection must also reassume
the same particles of matter as our own. It may be
so, or it may not be so; in any case the identity of
our risen body with our earthly body is beyond
question.

Another more cogent argument may be derived
from the Catholic doctrine regarding the veneration
of the relics of the Saints. According to the Council
of Trent, this veneration is based, not merely on the

past fact that they have been living members of
Christ and temples of the Holy Ghost, but also on
the truth that they are "to be raised and glorified by
Him unto eternal life." The relics we venerate stand
therefore in some direct connection with the glorified bodies of the Saints, which will live in heaven.

Scriptural language moreover, and the common
language of the faithful, connects the resurrection
with the opening of the graves and the sea giving
up its dead. Scriptural language connects our resurrection so closely with that of Christ that some
connection between the actual matter of which our
earthly body is composed and that of our risen
bodies is no doubt to be admitted.

It is true that our soul is the constitutive or informing cause of our body; it is, in scholastic language, its *causa formalis.* Through our soul the
matter of our flesh is a human body; yet the reason
why one man's body is not another man's (why my
body is one thing and yours is a distinct thing) lies
not in the fact that each is informed by a different
soul; there is a difference between the *material*
principles involved. It seems therefore that in some
sense, mere identity of our soul, informing matter,
would not constitute the body thus held, numeri-
cally the same with our previous one.

However this may be, the body we shall have in
heaven shall be really and fully the same body

which we have now. This body shall be a truly
human body, not a phantasm or an apparition of
varied colours and thin air, not an unsubstantial
cloud of vapour however lightsome and brilliant,
but a true human body. When Our Lord rose from
the dead, He appeared to His disciples, and they
feared because they thought they saw a ghost, but
He reassured them: "Touch and handle Me," said
He, "for a spirit hath not flesh and bone as you see
Me have." He ate and drank with them and He
allowed Thomas to put his fingers in the place of
the nails and his hand in the wound of His side.
Now Christ's risen body is the pattern of our own.

(2) THE GLORIFICATION OF OUR RISEN BODY

However human the risen body will be, it will be
none the less glorified.

This glorification of the body St. Paul describes
in Chapter xv of the First Epistle to the Corinthians: "It is sown in corruption, it will rise in
incorruption; it is sown an animal body, it will rise
a spiritual body; it is sown in infirmity, it shall rise
in power; it is sown in ignominy, it shall rise in
glory."

These inspired words of the Apostle of the Gen-
tiles, theologians have summed up in the four
words: impassibility, subtilty, agility and clarity.

Glorified bodies shall be impassible. No pain or harm of any kind can approach them. Sickness and frailty, hunger and thirst, weariness or exhaustion, are things that have for ever passed away, "neither shall the sun strike upon them, nor any heat," "neither shall there be mourning, nor crying, nor pain any more." "God shall wipe away every tear from their eyes, for the former things have passed away" (Apoc. vii, xxi). Capable as they are of every joy, they are not capable of feeling even the slightest hardship or discomfort, for they can suffer no more. Those amongst us who have known years of ill-health, those who can hardly remember what it is to be without some ailment, robust and strong, should often recall the truth: in heaven they can suffer no more. Being sown in corruption, a body subject to disease and pain, it rises in incorruption.

The second gift is called "subtilty." Having been sown an animal body, it will rise a spiritual body. It will never cease to be material, but it will nevertheless receive many of the powers and privileges of the spirit. We know from the Gospels that Christ on Easter morn left the tomb before the stone was rolled away, that He entered the upper room, the doors being closed. We know that Christ, even during His mortal life, walked on the waters, that His Body and Blood is present in the Blessed Sacrament all over the world. These things show what priv-

ileges God can give to a human body, yet leave it
material and human. He can, without destroying
the characteristic reality of the body, so assimilate
it to the spirit, so make it subservient to the indwelling soul, that it be a worthy yoke-fellow of the
immortal spirit.

It is sown in infirmity, it shall rise in power. This
is summed up in the gift of agility. The Lord has
created all things for the sake of the elect. *Omnia
propter electos operatus est Dominus.* At present,
limited as we are to this tiny globe of the earth, and
most of us to a small corner even of this world, we
do not seem to be masters in this universe, but
slaves. We do not seem to be lords of creation, but
rather the plaything of its forces. At present we are
cribbed, cabined and confined in the small area
which we can influence by our mortal body. The
time will come when the wide expanse of the universe, the remotest recesses of the starry skies, will
be accessible to us with the swiftness of thought, and
all God's world shall be our home. At present the
body is sluggish in its obedience to the soul, it is a
hindrance hampering the spirit in the fulfilment of
its wishes and energies; then the dominion of the
spirit will be absolute and the body will instantaneously react to all the saintly desires of the soul. It
shall rise in power. Its present feeble efforts to rise
to the demands made on it by the spirit shall be suc-

ceeded by a never failing power completely to fulfil
the behest of our higher nature.

Lastly: it is sown in ignominy, it shall rise in
glory. So lowly is the present state of our body that
many have thought it gross and contemptible, and
indeed at present it seems a mean thing, as a home
for an immortal spirit. Then it shall be clad in glory.
At the Transfiguration, Christ's face shone like the
sun and His garments were as white as snow, and
the disciples, overcome by the radiance of its beauty,
murmured, "It is good for us to be here." In the
story of the Saints, we sometimes read of a halo of
light surrounding the head of the Blessed. Those
are only indications and pledges of the glory to
come.

(3) THE LIFE OF OUR RISEN BODY

Having at the resurrection received our immortal
bodies, we shall possess them throughout eternity.

Therefore, heaven will provide an endless field on
which to exercise our bodily powers to the utmost.
Eyes with nothing to see, ears with nothing to hear,
feet with nowhere to go would be a useless gift of
God.

What scenes God shall provide for our eyes, what
music for our ears, what a Paradise in which to walk

in the cool of the evening, none of us can think. As children we pictured heaven to ourselves as a delightful garden, with shady groves and palm-trees. When we grew up we realised that the supreme joys of heaven are not those of the body, and perhaps we set all these things aside with a smile. When I was a child, I thought as a child. On second thoughts, however, even as adults, we conclude that, after all, heaven must contain the joys of sense, the joys fit and worthy for men and women with human, though glorified, bodies. We come to think that perchance our childish thoughts were less untrue than at first we supposed.

St. John in his Revelation saw the heavenly Jerusalem as a city with golden streets and walls and gates of precious stones. The Holy Ghost, therefore, did not disdain to use such descriptions of our eternal home. Even though these things be metaphors, they may be closer to reality than we thought. There must be physical glories in heaven of some kind, besides the purely spiritual ones. What they will be, God has not deigned to reveal, lest in our present infirmity we should let our minds rest more on the future joys of sense than on the Beatific Vision. He warned us that in heaven there is neither marriage nor giving in marriage. Though heaven may be likened to a banquet, yet we know that our body's need of food and drink can only be connected with our present humble state and be unknown in the land of immortality.

One thing, however, seems certain: that we shall have familiar intercourse with our fellowmen, that they shall be our companions and friends, and that we shall have speech with them as well as singing the praises of God with our lips.

No caste or class distinction shall stand between us and any of the myriads of citizens of the heavenly kingdom. Neither shall the greater glory of the higher saints repel those of lesser holiness; rather, it will attract them.

The supreme glory of Him, who in His human body, as well as in His soul, sits at the right hand of God the Father Almighty, will be the centre of all eyes in the court of His Divine Majesty, and the smile on the lips of Christ will be as the sun at dawn in springtide.

Nor will the Maid of Nazareth, who became the mother of God at the word of Gabriel, the archangel, be too great a Lady to be approached even by the humblest of the saints.

Thus happily mingling with the whole multitude of the heavenly host, moving amongst friends, moving amongst those who were on earth near and dear to us and then share our happiness, we shall glorify God in Christ, who is the author and finisher of our faith.

CPSIA information can be obtained at www.ICGtesting.com
Printed in the USA
BVOW020539140213

313181BV00001BA/2/P